•THE GUARDIAN SERIES•

THE

DARK WATCH

THE GUARDIAN SERIES
THE DARK WATCH

by Janifer C. De Vos

Illustrations by
Gwendolyn Babbitt

MULTNOMAH
Portland, Oregon 97266

Cover design by Bruce DeRoos
Edited by Deena Davis
Illustrations by Gwendolyn Babbitt

THE DARK WATCH
©1991 by Janifer C. De Vos
Published by Multnomah Press
10209 SE Division Street
Portland, Oregon 97266

Multnomah Press is a ministry of Multnomah School of the Bible,
8435 NE Glisan Street, Portland, Oregon 97220.

Printed in the United States of America.

Library of Congress Cataloging-in-Publication Data

De Vos, Janifer C.
    The dark watch / Janifer C. De Vo.
      p.   cm. — (The Guardian series ; bk. 3)
    Summary: Working with God's Guardians, Erin becomes
involved in a plot by which Demont, one of the broken ones from
behind the Purple Door, hopes to conquer Earth. Sequel to "The
Purple Door" and "The Silver Glass."
    ISBN 0-88070-418-7
    [1. Fantasy. 2. Christian life—Fiction.] I. Title. II. Series:
De Vos, Janifer C. Guardian series ; bk. 3.
PZ7.D4995Dar   1991
[Fic]—dc20   91-9026
                                                          CIP
                                                            AC

91 92 93 94 95 96 97 98 99 - 10 9 8 7 6 5 4 3 2 1

*Dedicated with love to
Linda, Lisa, Mary Ann, Sara, Dorothea,
and my five praying Pats
who have all heard the shofar
and come to the circle,
and
to my dad
who brought the joy of music
into my childhood world.*

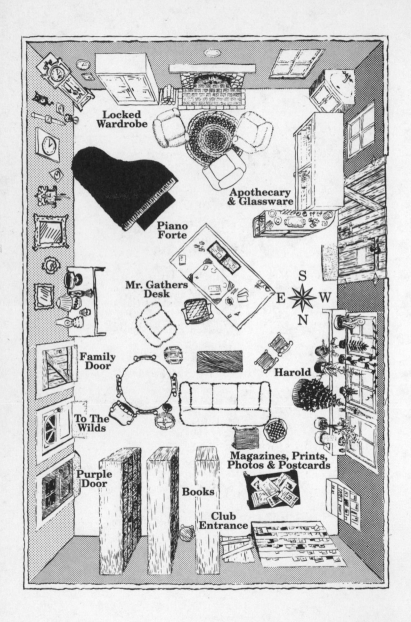

Locked
Wardrobe

Apothecary
& Glassware

Piano
Forte

Mr. Gathers
Desk

S
E ✦ W
N

Family
Door

Harold

To The
Wilds

Purple
Door

Magazines, Prints,
Photos & Postcards

Books

Club
Entrance

Contents

Prologue

The distinguished gentleman gazed into the clear waters of the heavenly pool. He smiled as another's reflection appeared beside his on the mirror-like surface.

"Penny for your thoughts, Dr. De Jong," the angel said.

"Well, Sam, I was just thinking about my granddaughter Erin. Maybe getting her involved in this Guardian business was a mistake. It's asking an awful lot of one so young . . . maybe we should have waited a few more years."

The angel shook his head, laughing, and patted Dr. De Jong on the back.

"Trust the King's timing, sir. He's never wrong! Oh, speaking of time, I'd better get going. I'm supposed to be on duty at 2:30, earth time. God go with you!" Sam disappeared in a whirling sparkle of light.

"God go with you, Guardians," whispered Dr. De Jong.

1
Drama and Beyond

ERIN GRIMLY STOOD next to her open locker, listening with interest to her friend Connie's plans for their music project.

"We could do a duet—you on piano, me on flute."

"That would be great."

"Maybe your dad could help us pick out some music and practice. What do you think?"

Erin slammed the locker door shut, balanced her books on one arm, and pushed her glasses up on her nose with her free hand. "I think it's a great idea except for one little detail: Dad left for a choirmaster's convention yesterday and won't be back until Friday night." The girls hurried along the crowded corridor to Intermediate Drama, their last class of the day. "But I know someone else who could help us—Mr. Sebastian!"

"You mean the Mr. Sebastian who works with you at Antiques, Antiquities, Inc.? I didn't know he was into music."

Erin looked at her friend and smiled. Noah Sebastian was "into music" more than Erin could even begin to explain.

The girls sat down in front-row seats in the

drama room. Erin loved the tall, old-fashioned wood-frame windows that ran along one wall. They gave the room character. She looked out one of the windows, happy with the thought that in just forty-five minutes she would be on the other side of the glass. As she started to turn away, activity in the courtyard caught her eye. "Uh oh," she said softly to herself.

"What's wrong, Erin? Forget something?" Connie looked across at her friend.

"Uh, no." Erin turned back to the window and stared out. Now the courtyard was empty. She sat back in her chair, pondering the implications of what she had seen.

Just as the bell rang, their drama teacher, Miss Sertell, marched hurriedly into the room with one more student right behind her. The student, Arnold Lorenzo, slid into the seat behind Erin and gave her long brown ponytail a tug. Erin reached for Arnold's kneecap without turning around and heard his sharp intake of breath when she made contact.

Erin really enjoyed drama class. Miss Sertell was a little on the strict side, but very funny, and the forty-five minutes went by quickly. When the bell rang, Erin and Connie got up together.

"Do you work today?" Connie asked Erin.

"Yes, so why don't you come to the shop at

around four o'clock. That's when we take a break. We'll get Mr. Sebastian to help us."

"Great! I'll see you then."

Arnold limped dramatically past Erin to the classroom door. "Erin Grimly, you've made me a cripple for life!"

Erin followed him out. "Arnold, who were you talking to in the courtyard just before class?"

"So, besides maiming me for life, are you also spying on me? What is this?" Arnold asked in feigned outrage.

"Arnold, I'm sorry if I hurt you. I just want to know who that was you were talking to . . . he looked like someone I know." *Boy, is he ever someone I know!* Erin thought to herself.

"Oh, he's just some new kid. He wanted to know where the science lab was, and I pointed him in the right direction."

"Do you know his name?"

"No," Arnold answered quickly. Too quickly.

Erin knew Arnold was lying, but she decided not to push it. She started toward her locker with Arnold following.

"So, I bet you'll go home and practice, and then, 'Hi, Ho! Hi, Ho! It's off to work we go,'" Arnold sang loudly. "What a drag. I've never been in that antique shop of yours. What's it like?"

Erin spun through the combination to her

locker and opened the door. "It's really cool. You should come and see, Arn. You'll especially appreciate what Mr. Gather has done to it since we used to play in that barn. I could give you a guided tour."

"I might drop by. It all depends on what the others are doing."

Suddenly Erin felt uneasy. She knew who "the others" were. They were gang members made up of older students from the high school up the street. "Arnold, I wish you would get uninvolved with those guys." She closed her locker and looked with concern at her friend. Arnold Lorenzo could be a real tease sometimes, but she had known him for almost her whole life, and she cared about him.

"Not to worry, E.E." He sounded confident, but Erin picked up on the falseness of his bravado. "I'll see you later, maybe."

Erin rebalanced her books and headed for home. She liked the walk. It gave her time to unwind and refocus for the rest of the day's activities. The usually pleasant walk turned a shade darker when she thought she heard footsteps following behind her once or twice. But when she turned around to look, there was no one there.

Once home, she chatted with her mother for a few minutes, ate some homemade oatmeal chocolate chip cookies with a glass of milk, and headed downstairs to her dad's studio to practice.

The upright piano sat in the corner of the paneled room under a high narrow basement window. The piano needed dusting. Erin's mother had long ago given up trying to keep her husband's studio clean, so now the dusting was done by Mr. Grimly, who rarely noticed the need for it. Erin got the dust rag from inside the piano bench and was just reaching to the top of the piano when she saw something move in the window over her head. Someone was standing on the other side of the window. She ran back upstairs, through the kitchen and out the back door to try and catch the trespassers. When she rounded the corner of the house, there was no one there. But there were several sets of footprints in the soft dirt around the casement. *Who had been standing there?* Erin wondered.

2
Duets and Delinquents

AFTER ERIN HAD finished piano practice with about a third of her usual concentration, she hurried up the hill of her backyard, anxious to tell Mr. Gather, her teacher, boss, and the owner of Antiques, Antiquities, Inc., about who she had seen in the courtyard at school and about the mysterious visitors outside her father's studio.

Erin ran up the path to the renovated barn and looked expectantly at the plaque on the front door. What would it be today . . . a poem to finish or a riddle to solve? The door would open only after the poem's missing word or the riddle's solution was stated by the reader. This time she saw:

Name this tune:

"Oh! How funny!" Erin was intrigued by this new development. She started to hum the first few notes, not sure the pitch was right, but

hoping the tune would still be recognizable. After three tries, she suddenly got it.

"I know what this is!" She hummed the rest of the melody. The treble clef and the notes vanished, but the door remained closed, and the command *Name this tune,* stayed on the plaque.

"It's in our hymnbook. 'Joyful, Joyful, We Adore Thee.'"

The door swung open, ringing the little bell that hung over it. As Erin stepped into the large room, a white long-haired cat came over to greet her. Erin bent down to stroke her luxuriant fur.

"Hello, Parenthesis. How are you? Where is everybody?"

The cat answered with a brief meow, sat down, and attacked some out-of-place fur on her tail.

"Hello . . . Mr. Gather? Noah? Is anybody home?"

Erin gazed around this place that had become "her" shop a few months before. The beautiful plants growing by the west window of the barn were a rich green in the afternoon sun. One of Erin's favorite places to go exploring on slow days was the row of bookshelves on the north wall that had been converted from cow stalls. But the adventure doors on the east wall were probably the most intriguing of all. The

Family Door and the Door to the Wilds were for rent if a customer was in the mood for fun. But the purple door at the row's end was one of Mr. Gather's newer acquisitions, one that was proving to be a continuing source of trouble. Mr. Gather kept it locked at all times. Even so, trouble had spilled out of it into the shop . . . and beyond.

Mr. Gather's prized clock collection ticked away, and the crackling of the ever-burning fire in the fireplace brightened the south end of the room. The flames were reflected in the glassware in the apothecary cabinet and the mirrors hanging on the east wall.

Where was everybody? Erin decided to go ahead and start her afternoon cleaning routine. Starting with the plants, she dusted leaves carefully, keeping clear of Harold the omnivorous conifer's poisonous branches. Then she moved on to the table of old magazines and photos. She had just picked up an interesting print of a young girl from the turn of the century, when she heard footsteps behind her. Turning around, she saw Mr. Gather midway between ceiling and floor, feet firmly planted on the steps of a staircase that was invisible to Erin.

"Hello, Erin. Already at work, I see." Mr. Gather joined her at the photo table.

"Mr. Gather! Guess what? I'm sure I saw

Demont on the school grounds today. And Arnold Lorenzo said he was asking the way to the science lab!"

"Hmmm. Well, Mr. Sebastian has been keeping close watch on him." Mr. Gather paused. "Erin, how did Demont look to you today?"

"Well, he was too far away for me to see him clearly, Mr. Gather. Plus, it was through a pretty dirty window. Oh, and speaking of windows, this afternoon when I was . . ."

Jungle drumbeats and wild animal shrieks and roars suddenly surrounded them both, as a grinning Noah Sebastian entered the room from behind the Door to the Wilds. "I've talked to the chief, Mr. G. He promised not to get so carried away next time. Hello, Erin!"

"Noah, could you help Connie and me with our music project this afternoon? We want to do a duet—Connie's a flutist. I told her to come about four o'clock, and maybe you'd help us then."

"Sure!"

"Noah, Erin thinks she saw Demont at school today."

"Yes, Mr. G. He's managed to connect himself with some local toughs who are giving him food and shelter at present," said Noah.

"Noah, if you're here now, who's watching Demont?" Erin asked.

"Not to worry. We've got him covered."

Erin started her dusting again as the two men walked away from her, talking shop business. She deliberately skirted the books, planning an extended stay there later, and gave the tables, chairs, and lamps a quick going over. Then she walked to the wood frames of the adventure doors and wiped along the edges and around corners. Stopping at the purple door, she thought about Demont. He had escaped into Erin's world from behind this door. Somehow, she, Mr. Gather, and Noah had to convince him to return there.

The sound of the jingling bell over the door broke into her thoughts.

"Hello! Erin! I'm here!" It was Connie, carrying her flute case.

"Hi! Is it time already?"

Noah came over to greet Connie. The three of them went to the pianoforte in the corner under the clocks, and Noah reached inside the piano bench for some sheet music.

"Here, girls, I happen to have this little number that you might be interested in. Let me play it, and you see if you like it." The soft piano sounds were suddenly joined by a flute . . . only there was no one in the room playing one. Connie looked puzzled and gazed searchingly around the room. Noah finished the piece.

"Well, what do you think?"

Erin tried to catch Noah's eye with her warning glare.

"I like it . . . but who was playing the flute part?" asked the mystified Connie who was still looking around the room.

"Well, you see, Connie . . ." Erin was hesitant to explain Noah's musical abilities, wondering what her conservative, commonsense friend's reaction would be.

Fortunately, Erin was interrupted by the front door flying open, causing the bell to ring madly. A familiar figure marched into the center of the room.

"Misssterrrr Gather!"

Mr. Gather walked calmly toward her. "Good afternoon, Dr. Banushta. It has been some time since your last visit. Things are going well, I trust?"

"We need to talk, Gather." Dr. Banushta pursed her lips and then stared in the direction of Noah and the girls. She gave no sign of recognition as she looked at Erin.

"Maybe I should go," whispered Connie. "This looks sort of serious." She picked up her flute case.

"Come back tomorrow, Connie, and we'll get this all together," said Noah. He walked Connie to the front door and opened it. "God go with you," he said.

Noah walked to Mr. Gather's desk and picked up some papers. Erin went back to her dusting, but she could hear the conversation at the fireplace clearly.

"I understand that Monty . . . er . . . Demont is presently here on earth." Miranda spoke with a sugary sweetness that made Erin's skin crawl. "He has something that belongs to me. I want it back." She sat up very straight in her chair, looking expectantly at Mr. Gather.

Mr. Gather said nothing.

"You know where he is . . . don't you?" Dr. Banushta squinted at Mr. Gather. "Just tell me where he is, and I'll get the pan—my property—back myself." She was annoyed with herself for her slip of the tongue.

"Miranda, we know he has your power panel, and we know where we can find him. What I am curious to know is just what exactly are the present capabilities of that panel?"

Dr. Banushta sighed and looked away from Mr. Gather. Then she faced him again. "All right, I'll spell it out for you. The power panel is broken, nonfunctional—at least it's not functioning as I had intended. I'm not sure what Monty might do with it now. I'm not entirely sure what it might do to him." She looked meaningfully at Mr. Gather.

"Demont collapsed last Saturday afternoon

while I was on watch," said Noah. "Could the panel be causing him any physical harm?"

Erin tried to remember how he looked when she had seen him earlier that afternoon at school.

"I'm not sure," said the scientist. "But I want my panel back, Gather. Since you are Guardian of the doors, and Demont is a resident from behind the purple one, it is really your responsibility—your *duty,* to get the panel from that delinquent Demont and return it to me. I'll be watching for an opportunity to get it back—one way or another."

But Erin understood something beyond Miranda's threats. She could hear it in her voice. *Dr. Miranda Banushta was afraid.*

3
Too Close for Comfort

ERIN HAD A LOT on her mind during school the next day. She had the uncomfortable feeling that she was being followed everywhere. She kept telling herself that she was imagining things, but she couldn't seem to shake the feeling.

"Hey, Erin!" Connie called down to her from the crowded stairwell. "What time should I meet you for practice with Mr. Sebastian?"

"Three thirty!" Erin yelled back. "Are you walking home today?"

Connie had made it to the first floor by now and stood next to Erin, books piled high in her arms.

"No, Mom is picking me up here on her way to the grocery store."

"Oh." Erin had not wanted to walk home by herself today.

"See ya." Connie hurried down the hall.

Erin squared her shoulders. "Okay, Erin," she said to herself. "You are a Guardian. You have the King on your side. There is nothing to be afraid of. Nothing." She thought about the Bible verses Mr. Gather had been encouraging her to memorize. There had been a good one for fear; what was it? "God is our refuge and strength, an ever-present help in trouble." She decided she'd say that one to herself all the way home.

Everything went fine until she turned the corner of her own street. Standing on the corner was a group of five or six boys. Erin recognized Arnold and Demont. The boys were arguing and didn't even notice her until she was abreast of them. Erin was startled to see how pale and gaunt Demont looked.

"Just get me what I want, and I will make you the most powerful gang ever." Demont sounded out of breath, as though he had been running.

"Why should we get you anything, Demont? You talk a good game, but I haven't seen you do much." A tall young man with long dark hair looked disdainfully at Demont. "You keep telling us that panel of yours can do great things, but you've only used it once."

"Yeah, man. Let's see more action here."

"Maybe that panel can't do anything now. Maybe Demont is bluffing."

Demont caught sight of Erin. "Hey, Grimly-thing! Come here!"

Erin kept walking and saying her Bible verse to herself.

"Grimly-thing has seen the panel work more

than once. She knows what it can do."

"Is that right, *Grimly-thing*?" The others in the group snickered. Erin had already seen the gang bully several other children in her neighborhood. She was afraid she was about to be their next victim.

She was well past the group now and only two houses away from her own. Resisting the urge to run, she walked faster, looking straight ahead.

"Leave her alone, guys."

Erin recognized Arnold's voice.

"Go home and practice, Grimly-thing. Don't forget to dust the piano today," a voice yelled out of the group.

Erin was shaking when she reached her own back door. She ran into the kitchen and through the swinging door into the dining room. Her mother was sitting at the dining room table working on her latest manuscript.

"Mom!" Erin started to cry.

Mrs. Grimly put her arms around her daughter and pulled her close. "Whatever is the matter?"

Between sobs, Erin told her mother about Demont, the gang on the corner, and the footprints around the basement window the day before.

"So this Demont character is from behind the purple door and has some equipment that belongs to Dr. Banushta?" asked Mrs. Grimly.

Erin nodded, sniffing.

"This story sounds much more exciting than the one I am currently working on. Mind if I borrow a few details for my next novel?" Mrs. Grimly grinned. The fear of the moment slid away from Erin, and she smiled back.

Erin's mother looked at her as though she had something important to say. Erin wasn't sure how to translate the vibes she was picking up.

"Erin, I need to say something to you, something serious, something I've had on my mind ever since you first met Mr. Gather and accepted your guardianship."

"Okay, Mom. I'm listening."

Her mother looked seriously into Erin's face. "Erin Elizabeth Grimly, there will be times in your life when you will be much more afraid or confused about things than you were today. You might even lose hold of your hope . . ."

Erin thought of her friend Señor Joshua Zayre, a Guardian in the sixteenth century who had lost hold of the hope of his guardianship and had temporarily taken off his Guardian ring. She never wanted that to happen to her.

"Always look to the King . . . always look up. People around you will disappoint you or mislead you, but God never will."

"That's almost exactly what Noah said to Señor Zayre!"

"And was it helpful?"

"Well, yes." Erin sat quietly, remembering her adventure behind the silver glass. "Mom, when do you think I'll get my ring? I've waited and waited. I've done everything Mr. Gather has asked me to do—memorized millions of Bible verses."

"Millions?"

"Well, a lot, okay? Did Grandpa De Jong have to wait a long time before he got his ring?" Erin's grandfather had been the last person in Erin's family to hold a guardianship.

"I don't know. But I do know that he wore it a whole lot longer than he waited for it, if that makes you feel any better."

The mantel clock in the living room chimed the half hour.

"Oh, I've got to go! I promised Connie I'd meet her at Antiques, Antiquities, Inc., at 3:30. Thanks for talking to me, Mom." Erin jumped up and kissed her mother before running out into the backyard and up the slope to the shop.

4
Practice Makes Perfect

CONNIE WAS ALREADY standing next to Noah at the piano.

"Sorry I'm late," Erin said, a little out of breath.

Mr. Gather came from behind the piano, a medium-sized metal key in his hand. "According to my latest acquisition, you are right on time!"

Erin only saw the key in his hand. "You've got a key that tells time?" she asked in amazement. "That would be a novelty item, not an antique!"

Mr. Gather laughed. "No, no, I was just winding "Grandpa" over in the corner." He reached deep into his pants pocket and pulled out a weather-beaten pocket watch. "But, according to this," he flipped open the cover, "you are only one minute late, which isn't late at all."

Erin joined Connie and Noah at the piano. Noah showed her the music he had played for them the day before.

"You've got to be kidding!" she said incredulously. "This looks harder than anything I've ever learned in my entire life!"

"There's a secret to this piece," said Noah.

"There's a repeating phrase throughout it, so, Erin, if you can master these first few bars, you will have mastered the greater part of the whole thing!" Noah turned to the music in front of him and began to play. Erin was relieved to hear only piano in the shop, and no accompanying orchestral sounds spilling from Noah's brain.

"You're right, Noah. I hear the same melody over and over again. Maybe I can do this. What does the flute part look like?"

Connie had the music in her hands and had been following along as Noah played. She was humming her part softly to herself, trying to sight read the notes on the page. "This is so pretty. Difficult, but pretty. We only have three weeks to master this, Erin. What do you think?"

With a sudden burst of confidence, Erin said, "I think we should go for it. Noah can help us if we get stuck and so can my dad. It's a beautiful piece. Play it once more, Noah, so I can hear my part again."

Noah started playing the opening lines, and the room filled with the sound of a full orchestra. Erin closed her eyes and put her hand to her forehead. Connie turned around and around in astonished bewilderment.

"You've got some stereo system in here!"

Erin looked at Noah who just played on as if nothing unusual were happening. After one last rousing crescendo, the piece ended.

"That wasn't a stereo system playing, was it?" asked Connie softly. She looked at Noah with wide-eyed disbelief. "How do you do that?"

"Noah just thinks about music and his brain waves spill over into the atmosphere. He is usually able to keep it under control." Erin looked with exasperation at Noah. He grinned back.

"Now, girls, what I think you should do is take this music home, practice it for a couple days, and then meet back here to start putting it together. I'll help you all I can . . . if you want me to."

Connie was still in shock from Noah's display of his musical gifts. She sat down on the piano bench next to him and stared into his face. "How can you do that? Did you learn it in college, or were you born this way?"

Noah just smiled.

"Play it one more time, please, Noah?"

Noah turned and faced the music again. Erin listened carefully as the music of piano and flute danced in the air, filling the shop with sparkling notes. The flute part added so much vigor that it was all Erin could do to hold still. It made her want to dance and dust and rearrange things.

"Oh, that was wonderful!" Connie looked thoughtfully at the flute case in her hands. "Well,

I guess I'd better get started." She took the music from Noah.

"Connie, be careful going home," Erin said. "I had an unpleasant encounter with Arnold's new friends today on the way home from school." Erin turned to Noah. "Noah, maybe you should walk her home," she said anxiously. "She lives right down the street from the shop."

"No, no, Mr. Sebastian, that's all right. I'm not afraid to walk home by myself. Good grief, Erin. You're getting a little spooked by this gang thing, aren't you?" Connie opened the front door and stepped into the late afternoon sunlight. "Bye, and thanks! Goodbye, Mr. Gather," she called over to Mr. Gather's comfortable form seated in front of the fire. "See you at school tomorrow, Erin."

The door clicked shut. Erin turned back to Noah and looked disapprovingly in his direction. "One of these days, you are going to get me into serious trouble, Noah Sebastian."

"Not to worry, my dear E.E., I have—Erin, what's the matter?"

Erin looked as if she was about to cry. "Arn calls me E.E. sometimes. Oh, Noah, I am so worried about him. He is messing around with people that he should stay away from." Erin quickly told Noah about her encounter with Arnold, Demont, and several others that afternoon on the street corner.

Noah led Erin over to the fireplace, and they sat down across from Mr. Gather.

"Erin, Arnold and Demont are both being watched by . . . um . . . uh . . . someone who has their best interests at heart," explained Noah. "If you get a chance to talk to Arnold, don't be afraid to say what's in your heart. It is imperative that we get Demont back behind the purple door soon and Dr. Banushta's power panel out of his hands."

"You know, Mr. Gather, when Dr. Banushta was here yesterday, she was afraid."

"Afraid, Erin? What do you mean?"

"Well, I can't explain it, exactly, but I know she was afraid of something. I could hear it."

Mr. Gather looked at her. "Well, keep listening, Guardian Grimly, keep listening."

5
The Gang Meeting

LATE SATURDAY MORNING, Noah walked purposefully down the street one block north of Erin's house. He left the sidewalk suddenly and plunged into the high weed cover of a vacant lot. Slowing down, he came to the edge of a small woods and stopped. He softly whistled the first four bars of "Joyful, Joyful, We Adore Thee" and waited for a response.

Another whistler blew back the next four bars. Noah walked a little further into the tree cover and stopped as another man met him.

"How's it going, Sam?"

"Shhh . . . You're interrupting a very important conversation. Come and listen."

Noah followed Sam a few more yards into the woods, and Sam motioned him to a hiding place behind some bushes. In the clearing in front of them six or seven boys of various heights and ages were sitting on the ground listening to the shouting match between Demont and another boy.

"I'm telling you, I can fix it easily. But I can't fix it with just any old piece of wire. It has to be a particular kind of metal alloy."

"Oh, come on, Demont. You've been saying that for a week. We took you in, gave you a place to sleep and food to eat, all on your word about this power panel, and Arnold's word that you are telling the truth. I, for one, am tired of waiting for you to do something. What do you say, guys? Have we waited long enough?" The young man looked at his friends. They all grunted, grumbled, and complained, but no one made eye contact, and no one came right out and took sides with Demont's attacker.

Demont looked at the other boys sitting around him, assessing their commitments. Then he squared his shoulders and stared defiantly at the other boy who had opposed him.

"All right," he said softly. "All right. So you want to see what the panel can do? I will show you. And when you have seen the power it has, even when it is broken, you will have new appreciation for its value . . . and for me."

The boys were silent. They looked at Demont, their curiosity tinged with fear. Demont took the panel out of his shirt pocket and pushed several buttons in a purposeful pattern. Then he pointed the panel at the youngster who had spoken against him.

Nothing happened. One of the boys in the circle laughed nervously. With sudden energy, the other boy grabbed the panel from Demont and started pushing buttons.

"Stop! You idiot! You don't know what you're—-"

The boy pointed the panel at the others one at a time with no obvious effect and laughed. Then he pointed it at himself. There was a sudden blinding flash of light, and he was gone. The panel dropped to the ground. The back cover fell off causing several components to tumble out.

Sam and Noah looked at each other.

"If that's what it can do when it's broken, I don't want to even think about what Demont could do with it if it were fixed," Sam whispered.

Demont scrambled to pick up the panel's loose pieces. The other boys got up and backed away from him, terror-stricken.

Demont studied the cracked panel in his hand, assessing the damage. He turned to the other boys, a gleam in his eye. "Don't you see? Don't you see what this could mean for us? No one would dare challenge our authority. We would be the gang above all gangs. Our enemies wouldn't come near us. We could rule everywhere!"

"Where's Bobby, Demont?" asked one boy. "Where did he go?"

"Is he dead?"

"I'm getting out of here. I don't want any part of this."

Three of the boys ran out of the clearing, right past Noah and Sam's hiding place.

The boys who were left stood near Demont, watching him carefully.

"Well, what do you say? Are you ready for positions of power, or will you run from me like the others?"

The boys looked at each other. Demont sat down on the ground and started tinkering with the panel. He flipped it over, exposing the interior, and the boys were surprised to see a soft green glow all around the panel pieces in Demont's hands.

"Why is it glowing, Demont?"

Demont laughed. "That's the power source. It is a beautiful green, is it not?"

The group was silent. Demont kept taking parts out and then snapping and fitting them back in again. In a sudden fit of impatience, he grabbed a stone and flung it at one of the other boys. "I can't do the repairs without the proper tools and equipment. If you don't get me what I want, all this power will be useless."

Slow smiles of accord passed between the other youths.

"Okay, Demont. We're in this with you. Tell us exactly what you need, and we'll get it for you."

"And what is your price?" Demont asked them shrewdly.

"When it's fixed, you'll use that thing to get

rid of all our adversaries." There was a cheer from the other boys.

"Let's shake on it, Demont." The leader of the remnant came toward him, hand outstretched.

Demont got up from the ground, both hands holding the panel. He pointed it deliberately at the advancing boy who immediately stopped dead in his tracks.

"Come any closer, and I'll send you the way of Bobby." Demont glared menacingly at the startled youth.

"Okay, Demont, I only wanted to—"

"No one touches me, not ever, for any reason. No one."

The gang members looked at Demont, bewildered.

"Now find a sheet of paper and a pencil so you can write down what I need. Some of the items will be easy for you to acquire, and some will be a bit more difficult to obtain. But if I am to succeed I will need them all."

The boys started searching pockets and policing the area for paper scraps and a pencil. Once these items had been found, they all sat down, and one of the boys wrote as Demont dictated to him. Several of the items were a mystery to the others, and Demont stopped to better explain. After almost an hour, the group disbanded, each with a piece of the list in hand, leaving Demont alone in the clearing.

Sam sat back on his heels, Noah sat against a tree beside him. "Well, what do you think? Can he really fix it?"

Noah looked into the clearing again, studied Demont, and turned back to Sam. "Yes, I think he can, if his comrades can get the proper tools and parts for him. And even if he can't fix it now, the panel has the capacity to harm anyone standing in Demont's way."

"Noah!" Sam's warning came just in time. A brilliant green beam swept in front of Noah's tree. He rolled to one side. Sam grabbed him by the shoulders and pulled him to his feet. The ground and brush smoked, showing the trail of the powerful beam. They both whirled around to spot Demont. Had the attack been intentional? Demont just stared vacantly at their hiding place, the panel poised in his hand. He raised the panel again and pointed at another target at the edge of the clearing. Nothing happened. He pressed more buttons and still nothing happened.

"Why won't you work? Why won't you work now?" Demont shook the panel in frustration, then put it to his ear as if to listen for an answer. "I'll repair you. I only need the parts. And I understand more than Dr. Banushta, so when I fix you, your capabilities will be greater, your power immense!"

Demont slapped the panel against the palm of his hand. "Hurry up, boys, hurry up with my stuff. I have work to do." He walked unsteadily to the edge of the clearing opposite Noah and Sam and looked into the woods beyond. He put his hand to his head, and then reached out to a tree for support.

"Hold on, Demont. You have work to do. It must be the atmosphere of this place that weakens you. Sit down, rest here." He slid his body down the trunk of the tree and rested against it, his eyes closed.

Noah and Sam watched him with concern.

"Is it the atmosphere, do you think?" whispered Sam.

"It could very well be part of the problem. But I'm sure a lot of how he's feeling is directly related to his exposure to the power source inside that panel."

"How much longer do you think he can last?"

"I'm not sure. But judging from the rapid rate of his deterioration in the week he's been here, I'd estimate that one more week will be about all his body can handle."

"Too bad we can't just grab him right now."

"You heard the Boss. We're to *watch* . . . not *catch*."

"Right."

6
Fence-Sitting

ERIN'S MOTHER WAS in one of her major cleaning moods because company was coming for dinner that evening, and Erin's fingertips were shriveled like prunes after several hours of floor scrubbing and furniture polishing. She was glad to be on her way to A.A., Inc. but she wasn't in the best of moods and didn't appreciate the challenging riddle the shop's front door presented to her.

This thing all things devours,
Birds, beasts, trees, flowers;
Gnaws iron, bites steel;
Grinds hard stones to meal;
Slays king, ruins town,
And beats high mountain down.

from The Hobbit *by J.R.R. Tolkien.*

"Oh, come on!" groaned Erin. "I'm not in the mood for this."

"Not in the mood for what?" asked a familiar voice behind her.

"Oh, hi, Arnold! I was just talking to the

door. You see, to get in, you have to finish the message written here. Today it's a riddle, and my brain just isn't up to it."

Arnold stood next to Erin and studied the plaque. He tried opening the door, rattling the doorknob. It was shut tight. He read the riddle again. "Well, I know the answer—Time!"

The door swung open immediately, ringing the overhead bell.

"How did you know that? I never would have guessed that in a million years!"

"I read the book."

"Did you come by to see the shop?"

"Well, actually, I'm not sure why I'm here. I was out walking and just sort of ended up on this sidewalk. Weird, huh."

Erin looked eagerly at her friend. "I'd love to show you around, now that you're here. How about it?"

"Yeah, okay. Give me the seventy-five cent tour." Arnold looked with interest around the room. He followed Erin from one section of the shop to another, asking questions and raising his eyebrows at Erin's answers. He was especially fascinated by Mr. Gather's collection of antique clocks. He was just about to open the glass door protecting the grandfather clock's swinging pendulum when Noah came into the room.

"Hello, Erin. And who have we here?" Noah

stepped forward to shake Arnold's hand. "You are Arnold Lorenzo, aren't you?"

"Right! How did you know?" Arnold shook Noah's hand.

"You and I have several mutual acquaintances, I think," said Noah.

Arnold tensed instantly. His smile was strained.

"Noah, Mom asked me to remind you and Mr. Gather about dinner at my house tonight," said Erin.

"No reminder needed. It's an event we are both anticipating with great delight," Noah said elegantly.

The front door bell jingled as another customer came in.

"That looks like one of your regular customers, Erin. Let me show Arnold around while you wait on her."

Noah turned to Arnold. "So, are you interested in timepieces, Arnold? I noticed you looking at the grandfather clock when I came in."

Arnold had the uncanny feeling that Noah knew his interests and motives better than even Arnold knew them himself. He turned back to the grandfather clock again and was surprised to see a large white cat staring into the clock cabinet.

"Nice cat. Yeah, I *am* interested in

timepieces." Arnold watched in amusement as Parenthesis swayed in time with the clock's pendulum. When she raised her paw and batted at the glass, Arnold reached down to pick her up.

"No, no, kitty. You'll—-what? Where did she go?" The persnickity Parenthesis had disappeared.

Noah laughed. "Don't worry, Arnold. Parenthesis has this habit of dematerializing when she's not in the mood to be petted."

"Dematerializing? Since when can cats dematerialize?"

"Parenthesis isn't your average earth cat. She came to us through the purple door."

Noah walked over to the row of doors in the northeast corner of the shop. Arnold followed.

"So this is the purple door," Arnold said softly.

"You've heard about it?" asked Noah.

"Uh . . . no."

"Arnold?"

"Okay," Arnold confessed, "I have heard a little bit about it."

"From whom?"

Arnold found himself answering before he had time to think.

"From this kid named Demont. He says he came through that door. I don't know any more than that."

Noah looked soberly at Arnold. "He's telling you the truth, Arnold. And we want to get him back behind the purple door again. When did you last see him?"

"I saw him after school on Friday. I think he's sick, physically, I mean. He's so pale. He passed out in my backyard a week ago. That's how I met him."

"I know. Arnold, have you seen your friend, Bobby, today?"

"No, I haven't seen him since yesterday afternoon."

Noah looked thoughtfully at the doors.

"Mr. Sebastian, do you know anything about the panel Demont has?" Arnold asked suddenly.

Noah's voice was stern, almost commanding. "Arnold, stay as far away from that panel as you can. It's leaking a dangerous substance. That's part of why Demont looks sick—from exposure to the leak."

"Couldn't you just grab him and throw him back behind there?" Arnold motioned toward the purple door.

Noah shook his head. "No. Demont has to decide to go back himself. The panel has complicated things. But all is under the King's control. So, we watch and wait for our opportunity."

"King? You mean like the King of England?"

"Nope."

Arnold looked confused for a moment and then the light dawned. "Ohhhh," he said suddenly. "I think I get it. This isn't a normal antique shop, is it? Who are you, really, Mr. Sebastian?"

Erin joined them as Arnold asked his question. She looked hopefully at Noah.

"I am a Kingdom worker, like Erin." He smiled at them both.

Several clocks behind them on the wall began to chime the hour. The grandfather clock bonged the loudest.

"Gotta go, Erin, Mr. Sebastian. Thanks for the tour. See ya."

"Arn," Erin called after him, "are you coming with your parents for dinner tonight?"

"Yeah, I guess." Arnold hurried out the shop door.

Erin was surprised by one of Noah's melodies unexpectedly filling the air. It wasn't exactly a happy tune, but it wasn't really sad either.

"What's that?" she asked.

"That is our friend Arnold's personal musical profile. What does it tell you about him?"

"Think it again." Erin liked playing this musical identification game with Noah. This was the first time he had asked her to interpret the music of someone she knew.

After listening to several bars, one word came to mind.

"Fence-sitting. He's fence-sitting. He hasn't decided where he stands about a lot of things."

"You're really getting good at this, Erin! Now, I want to give you the same warning I gave to Arnold: Stay away from Demont and his panel. The panel has been damaged and is leaking a harmful substance. The sooner we can get the panel out of his hands and Demont behind the purple door, the better."

Erin went back to her dusting job. She stopped in front of the clocks. "Time is weird, Noah."

"How so?"

"Well, think about it. We can't see it. It's different in different parts of the world, even in parts of the United States. It can seem like it goes really fast or really slow depending on what I'm doing. Present, past, future . . . all describe it. What do you suppose time would look like if it were a visible thing?"

Noah looked at Erin, puzzled. "You mean to tell me you can't see time?"

Erin thought he was joking at first. But she could soon see that he wasn't. "You can see time?" she asked in disbelief.

"Yes. Can't everyone?"

"No!" said Erin in amazement. "Noah, just exactly who are you and Mr. Gather?" She held her breath. Would he answer her question this time?

"Erin Elizabeth Grimly, I think you already know," said Noah softly. He disappeared in a whirling sparkle of light. She was left standing alone, mouth open, Parenthesis sitting quietly at her feet.

7
"Where There's Smoke..."

ERIN JOGGED DOWN the hill of her backyard and was greeted by her father. Mr. Grimly was wearing his favorite hawaiian shirt and bermuda shorts.

"Hi, sweetie. Busy day at the shop?" Erin's father looked up from the nest of charcoal he was symmetrically arranging in the rusty barbecue grill.

"No, it was a pretty slow afternoon for a change." Erin watched as her father expertly squirted lighter fluid over the charcoal brickettes. "Dad, why aren't you using the gas grill Mom and I gave you for your birthday?"

Mr. Grimly lit a match and dropped it onto the charcoal. As it flared to life, he and Erin backed away from the flames.

"I couldn't get it started, and I was afraid to wait much longer. An announcement came over the radio a little while ago about the possibility of a bad electrical storm coming through here in the next few hours. I didn't want to risk waiting too long and ending up with soggy, half-cooked chicken."

Erin ran up the back steps and found her mother busy in the kitchen. "Want some help, Mom?"

"No thanks, sweetheart. I think I have everything under control. Our guests should arrive shortly."

"Mom, are we going to eat outside?"

"There's so much more room on the patio," her mother said meditatively. "I know there's a storm warning, but I haven't heard any thunder, and the sky looks clear to me. We'll just have to play it by ear."

In another hour all the Grimlys' company had arrived. Mr. and Mrs. Smading and Connie walked over. The Lorenzos came by car, and just as the sky began to darken with the first storm clouds, Mr. Gather and Noah came down the backyard slope to the Grimlys' patio. Mr. Grimly had gone to pick up Grandma De Jong.

Although thunder rumbled in the distance, the grown-ups were too busy visiting to notice. But the flash of lightning followed by a tremendous crash of thunder directly over their heads got their attention, and large droplets of rain sent them dashing inside. Mr. Grimly had just forked the last piece of chicken on his serving platter when the storm hit full force. The others cheered as he sprinted through the rain and onto the back porch.

"Okay, Lord, now it can rain all You want!" Mr. Grimly said.

There were too many people present for

them to all sit down around the Grimlys' dining room table, so Mrs. Grimly quickly set the kitchen table for Erin, Connie, and Arnold.

"Let's sing the Doxology together as our blessing," said Mr. Grimly. He took the hands of the people on either side of him, and the others followed his example.

The harmony of voices raised in praise to God was wonderful to Erin. "Wow! We sounded just like a church choir!" she said and another great crash of rolling thunder punctuated her statement. The lights flickered, dimmed, and flickered again.

The three children loaded their plates with chicken, homemade potato salad, and Grandma De Jong's baked beans, and sat down at the kitchen table. Erin propped open the swinging door to the dining room.

"The chicken is great, Mr. Grimly," called Connie from the kitchen.

"Glad you like it, Connie," Mr. Grimly called back. "I—-"

Suddenly all the lights went out.

"What happened, Richard? Did you forget to pay the electric bill?" Mr. Lorenzo joked.

"Get the flashlight out of the drawer by the refrigerator, will you, Erin?" Mrs. Grimly asked. "I'll come get out our emergency candles."

"And your romance candles, too, Mom."

"Romance candles?"

"Yeah, you know, the ones you use to put Dad in a good mood."

The adults laughed. Erin didn't see what was so funny.

Mrs. Grimly sat back down in the dining room after lighting the last candle. "This just goes along with the other weird things that have happened today," she said ruefully.

"How so?" asked Mr. Gather with sudden interest.

"Well, this morning when I unplugged the coffeemaker, it didn't turn off! It kept sputtering and sizzling for another five minutes!"

"Then we couldn't get my new gas barbeque grill started," chimed in Mr. Grimly.

"You know, I had a strange thing happen with my vacuum cleaner this afternoon," said Mrs. Lorenzo thoughtfully. "Instead of sucking up the dirt, it spit it out all over the living room carpet."

"Right before Noah and I came over," said Mr. Gather, "the clocks in the shop acted in a peculiar manner. They all chimed different hours, and my grandfather clock chimed fifteen times for six o'clock."

The power of the panel? Erin wondered.

"Oh, speaking of time," said Grandma De Jong, "did anyone see the local news at six? I only saw the beginning before Richard picked me up. A boy from the senior high is missing. Bobby something. Arnold, is he anyone you know?" Mrs. De Jong addressed the question to the corner where Erin, Connie, and Arnold had pulled their chairs.

When there was no reply, Mrs. Lorenzo turned with irritation in their direction. "Arnold, Mrs. De Jong asked you a question . . . Arnold?"

Erin turned to the empty chair next to her. "He's gone!"

Mr. Lorenzo brusquely excused himself from the table, took a candle and walked into the kitchen. Mr. Grimly and Mr. Smading followed him. They all returned after a few minutes.

"He's not in the house," said Mr. Grimly to the rest of the group.

Mrs. Lorenzo started to cry. Erin and Connie looked at each other. What was going on?

"We are quite concerned about Arnold," said Mr. Lorenzo softly, putting a comforting arm around his wife. "He's gotten involved with a group of boys much older than he is, and this Bobby who disappeared today is one of the leaders."

"Is there anything we can do?" asked Mrs. Smading.

"No . . . no . . . just pray for him. Pray for us."

The electricity suddenly came on again, flooding the room with welcome brightness. Dessert was served, coffee was made without mishap and poured. Erin and Connie went to the back porch to see what the storm had done. Rain dripped off trees and roof edges. Erin could hear the splash of the gutter pipe. The cool evening air smelled clean.

"Where do you suppose Arnold went?" asked Erin.

"Probably to a gang meeting."

"Where do you suppose that other kid, Bobby, is?"

"I don't know."

"I'm really worried about Arnold. Those guys he's hanging around with are mean. I know Arn has his faults, but he's not like them."

"Yeah, not yet, anyway."

8
Wolf in Sheep's Clothing

THE NEXT MORNING'S short ride to church revealed more of the storm's damage. Limbs were down in almost every yard. Pine straw rimmed the street where high water had left it. Pulling into the church parking lot, the Grimlys were dismayed to see a jagged black streak down the side of the sanctuary's outer wall.

"Dad, what's that?"

"Looks to me like the sanctuary was struck by lightning."

They walked up the sidewalk together and rounded the corner to the church office. Pastor Pat was standing next to the open door, his hand grasping the doorknob.

"Good morning, Grimlys. How are you?" The tall angular minister smiled at the family.

"Fine, Pastor Pat," said Erin. "What's that mark on the side of the sanctuary?"

"We were hit by lightning last night during the storm. It knocked out the organ and the loudspeaker system, so we'll have to be old-fashioned today and use loud voices and the piano."

Erin started for her Sunday school class.

"Oh, Erin, I almost forgot. I had an interesting phone call, yesterday afternoon. It was from a lady who said she knew you, and she wanted to visit our church today. She said she was a scientist or something." Pastor Pat looked expectantly at Erin.

There was only one person this could be, but Erin couldn't quite believe Miranda Banushta had called her church with attendance in mind.

"Did she tell you her name?"

"Yes, it was Dr. Banished, or Famished, or . . ."

"Dr. Banushta?"

"Right! You do know who I'm talking about."

"Is she coming?" asked Erin half in dread and half in disbelief.

"Well, I told her that worship was at 10:00 and Sunday school at 9:00. She sounded as if she planned to be here."

The Sunday school tardy bell rang, and Erin left without further comment. She ran to class hoping Connie would be there to hear this latest piece of news, but Connie was nowhere to be seen. Finding her parents again after class, Erin walked with them into the quiet sanctuary, looking in every pew to see if Dr. Banushta was there. Mr. Grimly chose a pew about midway to the front of the little chapel. Erin sat next to the aisle, wanting to turn around and look every few seconds. An unexpected disturbance in the rear of the sanctuary caused several heads to turn, so Erin took this opportunity to look.

"I'll find my own seat, thank you,"
announced a familiar haughty voice. "And how
much are those programs? I suppose you have to
have one in order to understand what's going on
in here?" The words were sarcastic, demanding.

Erin watched the usher's surprised
expression. He had clearly never been asked the
price of a church bulletin before. Miranda
scanned the church and spotted Erin.

"Oh, Grimly! Good! I was hoping I'd see you."
She came marching down the aisle. "Well, move
over. I want to sit next to you."

"Yes, ma'am," said Erin. By now she was
acutely aware of several pairs of inquisitive eyes

turned in her direction. She and her parents moved down to make room for the large woman. Fortunately, the piano prelude started just as Miranda plunked down. She didn't say anything more to Erin. She studied her bulletin seriously, making pencil notations at all the places marked "Congregation will stand."

The Smadings slid in on the other side of Erin's parents. Connie looked wide-eyed at Erin when she saw who was sitting next to her friend. When the prelude was over, Pastor Pat came down the steps from the altar area and addressed the congregation.

"We welcome everyone to worship this morning. Please take a moment to fill out the registration forms at the end of the pews so we have a record of your attendance, and so that your neighbors can greet you by name at the end of the service. Please stay for coffee after worship. As you may already know, lightning struck our sanctuary last night and did extensive damage to our electrical system, so we're roughing it today."

Erin pulled the registration pad from the pew rack and handed it to Dr. Banushta. The woman took it from her and signed her name with a flourish. Erin was hoping she would fill out the address part, but Miranda left that blank.

The youth director, Barbara Bailey, came up next to make an announcement. "The Youth Rock Concert is this Friday night, folks. Several parents with earplugs have volunteered to drive." The congregation laughed. "We'll rendezvous in the parking lot at 6:30."

Erin and Connie gave each other the thumbs up sign.

Then the worship service began.

Everything went pretty well until the children's sermon. Leslie, Connie's little cousin, started crawling over everyone to get to the aisle so she could join the other children all sitting around Pastor Pat on the steps at the front of the sanctuary. Everyone moved good-naturedly so Leslie could get by. Everyone except Dr. Banushta. Miranda glared at the little girl so fiercely that Leslie started to cry. Miranda just crossed her arms and looked the other way.

Erin pulled Leslie up on her lap. "It's all right, Leslie. Don't cry," she whispered in the little girl's ear.

"You're mean!" said Leslie loudly, looking tearfully in Miranda's direction.

"Oh, good grief," said Miranda in annoyance. "Go on, then." She moved into the aisle so Leslie could pass.

Erin put the little girl down and pushed her past Miranda toward the waiting group of children.

Dr. Banushta sighed several times in visible boredom during the rest of the service. Erin wondered why she had come. It certainly wasn't to worship God or hear about Jesus.

When it came time to greet each other, Miranda stood stock still, staring forward, not shaking hands with anyone or accepting a handshake from anyone else. The only time Erin saw any change in Miranda's smug countenance was when the pastor gave the benediction.

"Now go out into the world in peace. Have courage. Hold fast to what is good. Return no one evil for evil. Strengthen the faint-hearted, support the weak, help the suffering, honor all people. Love and serve the Lord, rejoicing in the power of the Holy Spirit.

"May the grace of our Lord Jesus Christ, the love of God, and the fellowship of the Holy Spirit be with you all."

Miranda glared angrily, clenched her fists, and sniffed in surprise. She said something under her breath, but Erin couldn't hear what it was. Dr. Banushta followed the pastor down the aisle, marched past the surprised ushers, and went out the back door of the sanctuary.

All conversation at the coffee hour revolved around last night's storm, damage reports, and the area search for Bobby, the teenager who mysteriously disappeared the previous Saturday morning. Erin looked around for signs of Miranda and spotted her talking to someone at the far corner of the patio. Not sure she wanted to be seen, she started to turn away when she realized Dr. Banushta was talking to Mr. Gather. Lemonade in hand, she made her way through the crowd of chatting adults to her boss. She could hear Miranda's accusing voice.

"He's been behind the purple door. He knows their words: 'Strengthen the faint-hearted, support the weak, help the suffering.' And you won't let *me* go!"

Erin missed a few seconds of the conversation as she dodged two high schoolers who were shadowboxing.

"I saw it in the paper this morning, Gather," Dr. Banushta was continuing adamantly. "Front page, no less. You've got to do something."

"Dr. Banushta, I assure you we are doing everything possible. We know where the panel is. It will be just a matter of time before the situation is resolved."

"You'll have to do better than that, Gather. I want the panel back immediately. Just take it if you know where it is. Use force. I certainly will if I get close enough! Demont is your problem." Dr. Banushta turned on her heel and clomped to the parking lot.

Mr. Grimly came up to Erin, and the two of

them stood next to Mr. Gather.

"Good morning, Zacharias," said Mr. Grimly. "That didn't look like a friendly conversation."

"No, it wasn't, Richard. Did you have a chance to look at the paper before you came to church this morning?"

"Yes, but just the front page. Why?"

"What did it say?"

"Something about electrical and mechanical problems all across the southeastern United States. I didn't read much of it. The article mentioned the storm we experienced last night."

Mr. Gather didn't comment. Connie came running up.

"Erin! Are you going to the concert Friday night?"

"I want to. May I, Dad?"

"I don't see why not, especially since I'm one of the drivers," Mr. Grimly said teasingly.

"Oh, Dad, why didn't you tell me?"

"You didn't ask!"

"Dad!" said Erin in exasperation.

9
Wheel Deal

MONDAY MORNING'S WEATHER was a moderate rerun of Saturday evening's nasty storm. Thunder echoed down the halls of Erin's school, and lightning illuminated her classroom. Rain kept everyone inside for the day, and by dismissal time, student energy levels were running high. Fortunately, the rain was finally coming to an end when the bell rang. Children spilled out into the hallways and down the concrete front steps, a stiff, cool breeze and lingering moisture touched their faces.

Erin couldn't resist turning a few circles in the wind, arms outstretched as wide as possible. In the middle of her third twirl, a particularly strong gust of wind whipped past her, ripping one of her notebooks out of her grasp and sending its contents swirling into the low limbed trees and bushes edging the sidewalk.

"Oh, no! That's our Christopher Columbus project!"

"I'll help," yelled Connie who immediately began chasing flying papers.

The girls stepped onto the soggy ground behind the tall boxwood hedge. "Erin, here are a bunch. Check and see what you're missing."

Connie handed her the sheets she had just recovered and watched as Erin methodically reorganized them.

After a couple of minutes, Erin gave a sigh of relief. "I'm only missing the table of contents. It's got to be here."

The girls walked a little farther down the hedge, parallel to the sidewalk, Erin in the lead. She stopped suddenly, putting a warning finger to her lips. Connie stepped next to her, and they peered through the hedge at the group congregated on the sidewalk.

"Where have you been, Demont?"

"Did you figure it out?"

"Has any one heard any more about Bobby?"

An unsmiling Demont scanned the faces of the boys surrounding him. He sat down on a stone bench a few yards away from Erin and Connie and proceeded to lecture the group. Erin nudged Connie and pointed to Arnold standing on the fringe of the gang.

"I've been in the library today. And yes, I 'figured it out', as you so quaintly phrased it. All I need to finish the repair job on the panel is a small wheel, the kind one might find in a watch."

"That's all? Here, take mine apart. I can always steal, uh, I mean borrow another one from somewhere." The other boys laughed as one of the youngsters started to loosen the wristband of his watch.

"No, stupid, I can't use just any watch wheel. What do you think I spent the day at the library doing? Reading magazines? It took me that long to find the right watchworks with this size wheel in it. They don't make watches with this particular wheel any more. As a matter of fact, this wheel probably hasn't been made in about sixty years."

The other boys groaned. "Well, then, how are you going to fix the panel?"

"With the wheel," said Demont in growing exasperation. "Boy, you guys are dense."

"And where are you going to get the wheel, smarty, if they don't make this fancy-schmancy watch of yours any more?"

"I'm not going to get it . . . you are." Demont gave them all a superior look. "I know where to find a watch like the one I need. All you have to do is get it for me." He turned his attention to Arnold. "You have the best connections, Arnold Lorenzo. Get this wheel, and the gang will be forever in your debt."

Arnold looked mystified. "I have the best connections? What are you talking about? I don't know anybody with old watches."

"Oh, yes, you do. You know someone who knows someone who has exactly what I want."

Demont looked meaningfully at Arnold. The other boys looked at Arnold with new respect. Suddenly the light dawned. Old things. Antiques. Erin.

Demont didn't give him any more time to think. "We'll give you the rest of this week to figure out how you're going to do it, and then execute your plan. I've got to have the wheel by Sunday at the latest. The power source in the panel is starting to weaken, and I don't know how much longer it will last. I may need the wheel sooner, so don't dawdle. This meeting is adjourned. I have a headache. Does anyone have any aspirin?"

"I've got some other stuff that will make you forget all about your headache," said a persuasive voice in the back.

Demont went to talk to the possible source of relief, turning back for one final jab at Arnold, "I don't have to tell you what not doing what I've asked will mean . . . do I?" He started to laugh, mimicking the now missing Bobby playing with the panel the Saturday before.

The other boys walked away in little groups. Arnold was left standing on the sidewalk by himself, his hands clenched into tight fists.

When the coast was clear, Connie and Erin joined Arnold on the sidewalk. Arnold was so lost in his own thoughts that he didn't even notice them at first. When he did, he looked very guilty.

"Oh, uh, hi," he said lamely.

"Arnold, Connie and I heard everything. You're in over your head. You've got to get out of this group."

"Hey, don't tell me what to do, Miss Goody-goody."

"Arnold, we both heard what Demont needs to fix the panel. I'm smart enough to know that the perfect place to find an old watch like the one Demont wants is Antiques, Antiquities, Inc."

"Yeah, well, what if it is?" Arnold said defensively.

"Arn, you'd be stealing from friends! Someone could even get hurt . . . not to mention the damage Demont could do if he gets the panel working properly again. Doesn't any of this matter to you?"

Erin sensed Arnold's inner struggle. He was afraid, confused, unsure of what to do.

"Come on, Connie. Mr. Gather needs to know about this. Let's go." The girls headed for home.

"Fine," Arnold called after them, "I don't care what you do!" But in his heart he did care. He longed to run after them. But instead, he started walking in the opposite direction. He didn't see the man step out from behind a large oak tree and follow Erin and Connie.

10
Hedges of Protection

ERIN AND CONNIE hurried down the quiet side streets they always took on their way home. Older homes built of red brick, stone, and wood flanked the streets. High hedges served as natural fences between front yards and sidewalks.

"Connie, don't turn around, but I think we're being followed."

Connie obediently stared straight ahead. "How do you know?"

"I keep hearing more footsteps than ours. Don't you hear them?"

Connie listened intently for several seconds. "No," she shook her head. "Let's walk in unison, and then listen." The girls quickly fell in step with each other. Sure enough, there were extra footfalls between theirs.

"I told you!" hissed Erin.

"Now what do we do? We're another five minutes from your house and at least seven from mine."

Erin looked around for a place of protection. Looking down the block, she had an idea.

"Connie, at the bottom of this hill we always

turn left. The house on the next corner is Mrs. Chloetilde's. We could hide behind her hedge and then call for help if we need it."

"Good idea. Lead on, I'm right behind you."

The girls walked nonchalantly down the hill, turned the corner, and on Erin's signal, dashed behind Mrs. Chloetilde's hedge. It had obviously just been trimmed and didn't afford them the protection Erin had been counting on. They huddled low to the ground, leaning into the prickly short branches. They didn't have long to wait. Around the corner came Arnold. He stopped, looked confused, and then ran right past the girls' hiding place.

"Good! We've—"

Connie put a warning hand on Erin's arm. They both looked through the shrubbery to the street corner. Dr. Banushta had just rounded the corner and was walking briskly after Arnold. She, too, hurried past the girls' hiding place, never giving the hedge so much as a glance.

The girls stayed huddled behind the hedge a few seconds more.

"Are you expecting anyone else?" whispered Connie.

"No one else, . . . I don't think," whispered Erin.

They both got up slowly from their cramped positions and stepped back out onto the

sidewalk. Erin gave a big sigh of relief, and both girls broke into a nervous laugh.

They were startled out of their wits by a new voice. "I believe this belongs to you, Miss Grimly."

Looking back over the hedge to the spot where they had been hiding only a moment before, they were surprised to see a tall man smiling at them. He handed Erin a sheet of paper over the top of the hedge.

"My table of contents!" she said in amazement. "Thanks! Where did you find it? Aren't you Sam, the new guy who works at the library?"

"Yes, I am Sam, and I found your table of contents flying away on my way from ... to ... well, never mind. I thought you would want it back."

"Thanks, Sam. Do you live around here?"

"No, yes, ah, I'd better be going. You're on your way to see Mr. Gather, right?"

"Right! How did you know?"

"I've always been a very good guesser. See you around, ladies." Sam ducked down behind the hedge. The girls laughed and ran back around to their hiding place, fully expecting to find Sam there. But the ground next to the hedge was empty. The branches weren't even moving. It was as though no one had been standing there at all.

"This is too weird," said Connie softly, shaking her head in disbelief.

They walked along at a rapid pace and soon reached Erin's house. "Connie, would you go tell my mom I've gone to Antiques, Antiquities, Inc.?"

"Sure, Erin. Call me later and tell me what Mr. Gather said."

Erin hurried up the hill of her back yard as Connie stepped onto Erin's back porch. Half running, she came to the shop door, a message waiting for her as usual:

For He will give His angels charge
concerning you . . .
They will bear you up in their hands
Lest you—
Psalm 91

"Okay, I know pieces of this one." Erin stared thoughtfully at the words. "It's something about hurting your feet." The sign started to wink on and off. Then it gave her a few more words:

Lest you strike your foot—

"Lest you strike your foot . . . lest you strike your foot . . . against a stone!" said Erin triumphantly.

The front door opened, and Erin hurried into the shop. Mr. Gather was reading by the fireplace.

"What's up, kiddo? You're early today."

Erin told Mr. Gather about her afternoon. First, she related the gang scene she and Connie had witnessed right after school. Then she told him about their eventful walk home, including Sam's strange appearance and disappearance.

Mr. Gather listened carefully. He didn't say anything right away when she finished. Parenthesis jumped up in Erin's lap, purring loudly.

"Time for your snack?" Erin petted the cat from head to tail, stroking her affectionately.

"That boy who was missing was found this morning," Mr. Gather said suddenly.

"Where? Is he all right?"

"A highway patrolman spotted him wandering along the median of I-95, about 40 miles from here. He was very confused and very hungry, but aside from some second-degree burns on his face and hands, he's fine."

"I wonder how he got there?" Erin looked at Mr. Gather to see if he knew more than he was telling.

"I have it on good authority that Demont's power panel had a lot to do with his trip."

"What should we do next?"

"We aren't going to do anything. You are going to go home and start practicing. I want you to take a couple days off from Antiques,

Antiquities, Inc. Don't come in to work until Saturday. That should be enough time . . . " he said to himself. "You have music to learn for your duet with Connie, right? That should keep you out of trouble for a few days."

Erin admitted reluctantly that she did have plenty of work to do these last few weeks of school. But to not come to the shop until Saturday? That was like punishing her.

Mr. Gather understood the impact of his words on her and explained his request. "Erin, if you stay away from here, Arnold will have four days to decide on his own what he intends to do.

"Okay."

"God go with you, Guardian."

"God go with you, Mr. Gather."

Erin put the cat gently on the floor and rose to leave.

"See you Saturday." She walked slowly to the door, feeling a strong resistance to leaving.

"It's going to be all right, Erin," Mr. Gather called reassuringly from the fireside, "we're all under God's protection."

11
Friday Night Rock

EAGER ANTICIPATION OF Friday night's musical event kept Erin going the rest of the week. Every day she worked on her part of the duet that she and Connie were going to perform, and tried to stay occupied with other things so she wouldn't miss her time at Antiques, Antiquities, Inc. too much.

Friday night finally came. Members of Erin's youth group congregated in the church parking lot shortly before six thirty. Mr. Grimly and Barbara Bailey were the drivers for the night's excursion.

"Okay, folks, let's get going," said the no-nonsense, ever-in-control Miss Bailey. "Who is riding with whom?"

Connie and Erin were standing together next to Mr. Grimly.

"I'll ride with my dad," Erin declared firmly.

"I'm in Erin's car!" announced Connie enthusiastically.

Just then, Mrs. Lorenzo's station wagon pulled into the parking lot. Arnold got out, slammed the door, stuffed both hands into his pockets, and strolled, sour-faced, over to the group.

"Hi, Arnold! I wasn't expecting to see you tonight. I thought you had other plans." Miss Bailey looked at the obviously disgruntled Arnold.

Arnold stared at the ground. "Yeah, well, my mother strongly suggested I come with you guys instead."

Erin couldn't tell whether Arnold was mad or not. He kept staring at the ground, avoiding eye contact with any of them. They were all distracted by another car pulling into the lot, this one vaguely familiar to Erin, but not immediately identifiable. A young man with shoulder-length, curly brown hair got out, and walked over to Mr. Grimly.

"Good evening, Professor Grimly." He shook hands with Erin's dad.

"Hello, Ricky. Let me introduce you to everyone. You've already met Miss Bailey," Ricky shook hands with her nonetheless. Mr. Grimly turned, smiling expansively to the group. "This is Ricky Evans, one of my graduate music students. He is going with us tonight to complete a homework assignment for one of his classes."

"Hey, I'd like to have homework like that!"

The group laughed, and all greeted Ricky.

"Let's roll," commanded Miss Bailey.

"Ricky, why don't you and Arnold ride with us?" suggested Mr. Grimly.

"Sure!"

"Good, then the rest of us can easily fit in my car," Miss Bailey moved toward her blue Toyota. "Margaret, why don't you sit up front with me? Ryan, you and Peter can have the back all to yourselves."

In Mr. Grimly's car, the girls were busy quizzing Ricky while Arnold stared out the window at the passing scenery.

"I've never met a serious musician before," said Connie.

"Unless you count Mr. Sebastian," Erin reminded her.

"Mr. Sebastian has other work he does. Do you, Ricky?"

"Well, not right now. I worked at Disney World last summer, though."

"Neat! What did you do?"

"I was Q-tip master."

"What?"

"Q-tip master—I cleaned Mickey's ears!"

Arnold spoke up unexpectedly. "Did they let you have your hair that long when you worked there?"

"No," Ricky sighed in mock sorrow and said dramatically, "I cut my hair for Disney."

The concert was being held in a large field just outside town. Hundreds of teenagers were already streaming onto the field in front of a large stage. The city's lights twinkled in the background. Mr. Grimly and Miss Bailey noted the arrangement approvingly. The tuning up and testing had already started. The group found a place to stand and watched the crowd grow around them. Excitement was running high.

Ryan, one of the older boys in the group, turned to Mr. Grimly with a serious expression on his face. Lifting one eyebrow, he cocked his finger at Mr. Grimly and asked, "Have you ever done drugs?"

"Ryan!" said Erin, Miss Bailey, and Peter all at once. Then they all started laughing. Mr. Grimly looked in puzzled confusion at Ryan and the rest of the group.

"Dad, that's Ryan's favorite sentence. And he asks it to people everywhere—*poor, innocent, unsuspecting people.*" Erin glared now at the gleeful Ryan.

The lights on stage blazed suddenly. All eyes turned to the front.

"Ladies and gentlemen, there will be a slight delay. No more than ten minutes, I promise." The announcement was greeted with a chorus of groans. "We're experiencing electrical difficulties up here. I'm sure you wouldn't want anybody in Armageddon to get zapped and meet the King tonight."

The crowd laughed, and the spotlight on the announcer went off.

"What's the matter, Peter? You're much quieter than usual tonight."

"My teeth hurt. I got my braces tightened at the orthodontist today, that's all."

"Did you know," broke in Ryan in his serious, scientific voice, "that petroleum is used in toothpaste? That we are, in fact, brushing our teeth with dead dinosaurs?"

"Ryan, that's disgusting!"

Ryan turned to Miss Bailey, stared her in the eye and said, "Have you ever done drugs?"

Miss Bailey stared back at him and said with a straight face, "Teenagers—you can't live with 'em and you can't shoot 'em!"

Even Arnold cracked a smile at that one.

"Miss Bailey, your JLR just improved," commented Ricky.

"JLR?"

"Your joke-to-laugh-ratio!"

The band suddenly yelled out a greeting, and the music swept over the crowd as Armageddon opened the evening with their version of the Doxology. Erin looked over to see how her dad was taking it. He seemed to be enjoying himself. Then she looked at Arnold. He was nervously looking over his shoulder, and even turned around several times as if he had been hit by something.

By the third song, everyone in Erin's group

87

was cheering and clapping in time to the music except Arnold, who wasn't joining in at all. His eyes kept scanning the crowd with a tense expectancy.

"Arn," Erin yelled above the din, "are you looking for someone?"

"No, no," but his eyes kept searching the crowd. "Erin, look, I've got to talk to you."

Arnold pointed to the concessions stand and cupped his hand around an imaginary drink. Erin got the message and followed him through the crowd after letting her dad know where she was going.

Arnold moved nervously through the crowd, glancing furtively in all directions. They joined the long line of other young people and adults waiting for service.

"Arnold, what is the matter?" Erin asked, a little exasperated.

"They've been following me everywhere," he answered nervously. "I haven't seen any of them here, though."

"Who has been following you?"

"The gang."

"The gang? Why?"

"I don't know why. E.E., could I come with you to Antiques, Antiquities, Inc. tomorrow? I want to talk to Mr. Gather or Mr. Sebastian about all this. That's all. Honest."

Erin didn't know what to say. She knew for sure that Arnold was sincerely afraid. Some pushing in the line distracted her. She turned to see what the commotion was about.

"Well, well, well, if it isn't Arnold with a little girlfriend. How nice." Two boys Erin recognized from the gang shoved their way next to them.

"How ya comin' on that project for Demont, Arnold? Demont sent us to remind you that you only have a couple of days to get what he wants." The boys moved in closer to Erin and Arnold. One of them grabbed the front of Arnold's shirt with one hand and twisted it. He was about to say or do more when several adults intervened.

As the two gang members backed off, one called out a warning, "Don't foul up, Arnold, my man. They found Bobby, but I doubt very seriously that they'll ever find you if you mess up."

Arnold was visibly shaken. He and Erin left the line without their drinks and started back for the group's place on the field.

"I'll be at the front door of the shop at three o'clock tomorrow. I'll wait for you." Erin looked into Arnold's pale face. "Don't worry, Arn, it's going to be all right. Mr. Gather and Mr. Sebastian will know what to do."

12
Battle Stations

SATURDAY MORNING ERIN woke up with a headache and a sore throat. Her mother took her temperature, gave her a big glass of orange juice, and sent her back to bed for awhile.

Erin sat in her bed sipping juice, thinking. Parenthesis unexpectedly materialized next to her hand. Erin stroked the cat and watched as she moved in closer to get more petting.

"You are such a funny kitty," Erin said aloud. She winced. It hurt to talk. It also hurt to swallow the orange juice. She frowned and went back to thinking. *Arnold, Arnold, what do I do about Arnold?*

Her dad suddenly appeared at her bedroom door yelling and jumping up and down.

"Dad! What's the matter?" Erin croaked.

"Nothing," Mr. Grimly said innocently. "I was just imitating last night's band. Don't you recognize me? I'm the drummer!" And he started his wild gyrations again.

Mrs. Grimly pushed past her husband and came to sit on Erin's bed. She pulled Parenthesis into her lap, tickling the cat under her chin.

"Should we call Mr. Gather and tell him you

won't be coming in today?"

"No!" Erin protested and then put her hands to her aching throat.

"Such enthusiasm for work! I wish my students got that excited about my classes!" Mr. Grimly came and sat next to his wife.

Erin looked at her parents. She knew her mother wouldn't let her go to the shop if she were really sick. But she had to. She just had to.

"Mom, Dad, I promised Arnold I'd meet him at the shop at 3:00, so he could get in to see Mr. Sebastian. It really matters. He's in big trouble with the gang that Mr. and Mrs. Lorenzo were telling you about last weekend." Erin settled back on her pillows and looked at her parents.

"Can't Arnold get in by himself? Doesn't the shop have a front door like most places?" Mr. Grimly gazed quizzically at Erin.

Mrs. Grimly answered for her. "No, Richard, the shop doesn't have a front door like we are accustomed to using."

"You know, I really should go over there once. Antiques, Antiquities, Inc. sounds like the most intriguing place."

"Erin, stay in bed this morning, gargle when I tell you to, and we'll see how you feel this afternoon." Mrs. Grimly patted Erin's hand. Her parents left her alone with her thoughts.

Erin was worried. Worried about Arnold. Worried about 3:00. She wasn't at all sure why, she just knew she was.

After lunch, she fell asleep, and when she woke up at 2:30, she found she could swallow without too much pain. She got up and walked to the kitchen where her mother was reading one of her cookbooks. Erin went over and put her arms around her.

"Mom, I feel better," she said.

"Good! You don't feel as warm any more, either." Mrs. Grimly felt Erin's forehead and hands.

"So, can I go to meet Arnold?"

"Yes, just take it easy at work today. No going through the Door to the Wilds, or anything strenuous."

"Yes, ma'am!"

Erin dressed hurriedly, zipped out the back door, down the steps, and up the sloping hill of her backyard. She crossed over into the field where the antique shop was nestled in the tall, early summer grass. Looking at her watch, she saw she was a few minutes early. She looked in all directions for Arnold. Seeing no one, she looked at the door to see what was written there for her to figure out today. Much to her surprise, the brass plaque which always held a message for her was blank.

"Hey, what's the deal here? I—"

The sound of running feet startled her. It was Arnold, galloping toward her, shouting something that she couldn't understand. As he got a little closer, she saw four other boys behind him, one of them sprinting ahead suddenly, gaining on Arnold.

"Open the door!" Arnold bellowed.

"Emergency—Erin Grimly here. Open please." Erin had her hand on the doorknob before she had finished speaking. The door swung open. She rushed inside, Arnold right behind her, and slammed the door right in their pursuer's face. The other boy started pounding on the door, demanding entrance.

Arnold leaned forward, his hands on his knees, his breath coming in short gasps. When he started to straighten, Erin could see that his hands were shaking.

Mr. Sebastian had seen everything from the vantage point of Mr. Gather's desk, and he now came around to Arnold's side, concerned for the boy.

Arnold looked up at Noah. "Mr. Sebastian, I need to talk to you." His words came out jerkily.

"Catch you breath, Arnold. Then we'll talk." The three of them went to the chairs by the fireplace. Mr. Gather joined them. Arnold quickly regained his composure and told his story.

"I'm afraid of getting hurt," he said at the

end of his monologue. "That's for sure, but I don't want to have a part in helping Demont fix that panel. Who knows what he could do with it."

Mr. Gather sat thoughtfully in his chair. He was about to say something when more noise outside caused them all to look at the front door. They could hear yelling; it was a woman's voice this time.

"That's Miranda!" said Erin, recognizing the screeching tones.

Noah got up and walked to a window overlooking the front of the shop. "You're right, Erin. And she has company."

Noah pulled the door open, and Miranda Banushta barged into the room holding Demont in a chokehold.

"Let go! You're hurting me! I can't breathe! I—can't—breathe!" Demont did indeed look as though he were struggling to get a good breath of air. Dr. Banushta loosened her grip on the boy, and he slumped to the floor in a faint.

"I wasn't holding him that tightly," Miranda spat defensively. "He's probably faking."

Mr. Gather squatted down next to the boy and took Demont's wrist, gently feeling for a pulse. Then he put his hand on Demont's forehead. "Can you hear me, son? Demont, can you hear me?"

Demont's eyes flickered open. He rolled

96

away from Mr. Gather's hands.

"Demont, you're really hot. Tell me how you feel. Do you have pain anywhere?"

The boy closed his eyes again, rolled over on his side and pulled his knees to his chest. Erin was unexpectedly aware of a message coming from Demont. She closed her eyes so she could concentrate better. She kept hearing a repetition of soft moans and the same word over and over again. She listened harder. Suddenly, she had it.

"Home! Demont wants to go home! Back behind the purple door!"

Demont raised his head from his knees and nodded at Erin. His face was tear-stained. His eyes closed again, and he slumped to the floor.

"That's out of the question," blurted Miranda. "My power panel's dysfunctioning has caused various problems locally—"

"And nationally," interrupted Arnold.

"Yes, and nationally, and I strongly advise against using the doors for several days—at least until I can stabilize the panel energy fields." Dr. Banushta moved purposefully to the prone Demont. She had every intention of taking the panel from him now, by force if necessary.

"Okay, Demont. I've absolutely had enough of all your little tricks. Give me my panel—NOW, sir. Do you hear me?" She poked his shoulder blades with one of her long fingernails. The boy cowered in uncharacteristic submission.

With a suddenness that surprised them all, Demont jerked the panel out of his pocket and held it tightly.

"No!" he screamed. "No! You can't have it. You dropped it, and now it's mine. Mine!" He looked like he was going to pass out again.

Dr. Banushta lunged forward and made a grab for the panel. Demont went toward the adventures doors in the northeast corner of the room.

"Noah, stop him!"

Demont moved unsteadily toward the purple door's burned frame. He threw himself in the direction of the door in one last desperate attempt to escape Miranda's reaching hands. He didn't even try to open it. He crashed right through the door's wood and glass, leaving the others frozen in disbelief.

"Here we go again," Noah muttered.

13
Door Dilemma

ERIN, MR. GATHER, Noah, and Dr. Banushta gathered around the splintered door which swung crazily, hanging by one brass hinge.

"There's blood on the wood."

Erin could feel warm air blowing into the room from the gaping hole. She peered anxiously into the purple passage beyond the door frame. One would never guess there was another world beyond the frame.

"Well," Mr. Gather said, "we're getting closer to completing our assignment. At least Demont has gone back behind—or, more accurately, through—the purple door of his own free will."

"With my power panel, Gather!" Dr. Banushta picked up a china plate on the sale table beside her and hurled it angrily against a wall. "With my panel!"

"Madam, please!" Mr. Gather turned to the scientist in dismay.

"I want my panel back!" Miranda spoke through gritted teeth.

"Couldn't you just go and get it?" Arnold asked timidly, ready to duck if Miranda decided to throw anything else.

"No! Absolutely not! Haven't you been listening, boy? It's too dangerous." Miranda snarled in his direction. "Given the panel's present state of dysfunction, there's no way to know when we could safely enter the world beyond the purple door, and I, for one, most certainly would not wish to be a part of the adventure party if the timing were wrong."

Erin looked at the adults around her and then at Arnold. She swallowed and grimaced. Her sore throat was coming back. Noah watched her with concern.

"What do you mean?"

"I mean exactly what I said!" Dr. Banushta answered impatiently. "There is no safe way to use the doors until I've either repaired or neutralized the panel. And now, thanks to your habitual interference, I can do neither one. All is lost!" Miranda reached for a sugar bowl to punctuate her last statement. Noah quickly moved to take it out of her hands.

"How much more damage could Demont do

with the panel as it is now?" Arnold asked.

"I'm not sure," answered Dr. Banushta shortly. "It's not going to matter anyway in another hour or so."

"Why do you say that?" asked Erin in alarm.

"Never mind. Just trust me. It won't matter." Miranda walked over to the chairs by the fireplace and plopped down, drumming her fingers on the arm of the chair.

Erin felt a furry nudge against her legs. Looking down, she saw Parenthesis.

"Explain your statement, Dr. Banushta," commanded Mr. Gather. "Why won't it matter in an hour or so?"

Miranda slapped the chair suddenly and looked at them all out of blazing eyes. "Think! Think! Demont has been exposed to earth's atmosphere and the panel's leakage for two weeks now. From the looks of him before his dramatic exit, I'd say he's just about taken all the exposure he can handle."

Erin looked incredulously at the unconcerned Miranda. "You mean he's going to die in an hour if he doesn't get away from the panel?"

Parenthesis left Erin's side and walked to the purple door. She sat there and meowed loudly, distracting Erin for a moment.

"Yes." Miranda yawned. "It's his own fault. He should have given me the panel when I asked for it." She turned on Arnold. "And you deserve some of the blame, too! If you'd done what he asked, proper repairs could have been made."

Erin was only half listening. Parenthesis started pacing back and forth in front of the purple door.

"Parenthesis would sure know when it was safe to go through the purple door," Erin said to Mr. Gather and Noah. "After all, she's from behind it."

They watched intently as Parenthesis struck out with her paw at the purple door. Suddenly, she disappeared. Then she reappeared at Erin's feet, meowing, and running back to the purple door, only to disappear again.

Erin and Noah looked at each other and simultaneously moved to the purple door.

"Okay, Parenthesis, we're coming."

"You're both crazy. There's no way to be sure the door is safe. Who knows where or how you might land?"

"Oh, ye of little faith," chided Noah.

He and Mr. Gather quickly pulled away bits and pieces of the broken door frame until there was enough room for Erin and Noah to get through without getting snagged.

"Okay, Erin, how does this work?"

"Well, last time I fell a long way down, and an angel, Protaimeus, caught me before I became a permanent part of the landscape."

Noah looked past the entrance. "I can see something to walk on. Why don't we step in together and see what happens?" He reached out and took Erin's hand. She stood beside him.

"Ready?"

"Ready!"

14
The Purple Door

WITH HER FIRST step, Erin felt the atmosphere changing. A warm dry wind swirled around her. She sensed a distancing of herself and Noah from the shop. Stone walls rose on either side of them. Erin could easily touch the ceiling. Noah was slouching next to her, trying to avoid bumping his head.

"This sure beats the free fall Miranda and I took through the door the last time."

Music of Vivaldi's *Four Seasons* echoed around them. The "Winter" score was dark and foreboding. "Noah, it's dark enough here without you adding to the atmosphere," Erin scolded.

"Sorry. How about "Autumn?"

"Okay."

The violins gave encouragement to their careful steps through the winding tunnel.

"It's so dark . . . I wonder where we are?"

"When you came back to the shop after your first visit behind the purple door, how did it work?"

"Protaimeus brought me to a door in a cliff. I walked through it and down a kind of hall, and then, bingo, I was back in the shop with you and

Mr. Gather."

They walked along a little further.

"Erin, when we—"

Noah's words were cut short by a menacing rumble and shaking of the walls around them.

"Earthquake?" squeaked Erin.

"Come on, I see light ahead." Noah pulled her forward. Clouds of choking dust surrounded them. Noah guided her through showers of dirt and smaller pebbles.

"Come on! We're almost there!"

Erin could just make out a dimly lit opening several yards ahead of them. In just a few seconds they emerged into fresh, warm sunlit air. When they turned back to look at the place from which they had come, rocks and clods of dirt rolled out in clouds of fine dust.

"I hope Parenthesis is safe," said Erin. She let go of Noah's hand and started brushing off some of the loose dirt on her clothing and hair.

"Erin!"

Noah was kneeling just beyond the cave entrance. Demont lay face down on the pebbly ground. Noah gently turned him over.

"He's bleeding."

"His head . . . it looks bad." For a second Erin thought she was going to be sick.

"Erin, I need something to stop the bleeding. Do you have a handkerchief, a bandana, something I could use?" Noah propped the unconscious boy against the cliff.

Erin pulled the scarf she was using as a belt through the loops of her jeans and handed it to Noah. Within a few seconds Noah had expertly bandaged Demont's head. Noah came up empty-handed after a search of Demont's pockets for the panel.

"Where could it be?" Noah said under his breath, his eyes urgently scanning the ground around him.

"Noah, he's slipping away from us. I can feel it—I think he's dying." Erin shaded her tear-filled eyes against the desert sun and desperately called, "Protaimeus? Pro-tai-me-us!"

When she turned back to Noah and Demont, Protaimeus was bending down to pick up Demont's limp body. There was no time for a glad reunion or introductions.

"I must take him to the circle. I only hope it is not too late." Protaimeus picked Demont up and ascended into the air above them. "Follow the path of dark stones. You will find us."

Erin searched for signs of a trail of dark stones. She spotted them almost immediately and called to Noah, "Here, they're over here."

"Okay, Erin, we'll come back and search for the panel later."

The desert sands stretched away from them

in all directions. Erin had to walk fast to keep pace with Noah's long legs.

Noah had just begun a new serenade when the music was interrupted by the mournful wail of a distant horn. It echoed hauntingly from stone to stone.

"What was that?" Erin shivered.

"A *shofar*—a ram's horn. It's a call to battle or to worship."

They heard feet scurrying behind them. Turning around, they saw a dark-skinned boy in flowing dress coming toward them.

"You hurry, you hurry, please. Pro says to hurry."

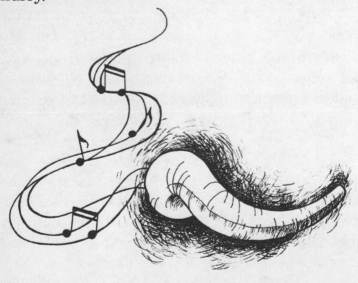

15
The Dark Watch

ERIN AND NOAH half walked, half ran after the little boy who nimbly navigated the path in front of them. Wisps of brown hair peeked out from under his turban, and his long robe brushed the ground as he trotted along.

The wail of the shofar floated across the desert sands, echoing all around them again. The boy turned around and regarded them with serious brown eyes.

"It is not well with your friend," he said. "The shofar is calling everyone to prayer."

"Where are we going?" asked Erin after following their small guide past numerous craggy rocks and up and down several large sand dunes.

"To the prayer place," the boy said matter-of-factly. "I am allowed to sit in the circle now because I have heard the Almighty's voice and answered His call." The youngster spoke with glad confidence. Before Erin could question him, they rounded a large outcropping of rocks that overlooked a flat, sandy plain. In its center, Erin saw bowed figures, some wearing turbans, some bare-headed, some women with long hair wound around their heads, all gathered around Demont. Over to one side, another group of people sat in respectful silence.

"Erin," whispered Noah, "look who the little girl is holding—over in the corner."

Erin looked and started to chuckle. "That cat!" There sat Parenthesis, enjoying the devoted attention of the little one who was scratching her ears and tickling her chin.

Protaimeus rose from the praying circle and came to greet them. He nodded his thanks to their young guide who went to join the others.

"Come, your prayers are needed."

As they approached the group, Erin heard soft voices. Some of the people in the group sat with hands folded and heads bowed. Others lifted their faces heavenward, palms turned up in a posture of praise.

Protaimeus motioned for them to sit down. There was such reverence in the air that Erin felt like she was in church. She had just closed her eyes and bowed her head to pray when she thought she heard her name called.

"Lord, keep Erin under Your protection."

Erin looked up, startled. The voice was her mother's! Looking around and seeing only other bowed heads, Erin resumed her own praying when she heard another familiar voice quite close to her.

"Merciful God, we give You thanks for Your constant presence with us. We pray for those in crisis today, and especially lift . . . "

This voice belonged to Pastor Pat!

"Noah?" she whispered. "I just heard my mom and Pastor Pat!"

Noah, kneeling beside her, turned, acknowledged her statement with a smile and a nod, and went back to his praying.

Demont lay very still. Erin was afraid that they were indeed too late. A young woman in the group moved to get him to drink something. A wizened elder gently put a compress on his head.

Erin closed her eyes again and began interceding for the boy. This time when she heard a voice she knew, she just listened quietly.

"Give her strength for today, Lord," said Grandma De Jong. *Was she praying for Mom?* Erin wondered.

It comforted Erin to hear these familiar, much-loved voices praying right along with her. She sighed, and tried to continue her own praying. But the next voice she heard was her Grandpa De Jong.

"Keep Erin looking up, and Demont holding on."

Before she could react, Demont began struggling to sit up.

"The panel! It's . . . I've . . . " He fell back and didn't move.

Erin felt a hand on her arm and looked up into Noah's face. He drew her out of the circle to the edge of the plain. "We should go back and look for the panel one more time. It must have fallen out when he hit his head. I don't want anyone else to be hurt by that thing. Are you up to it? How's your throat?"

Erin swallowed a test swallow. "It's fine!"

"You must have gotten caught in the prayer fallout," Noah laughed. "Come on, it's a bit of a hike back. Any music requests?"

"How about 'Climb Every Mountain'?"

16
In Hand and Out Again

THEY WALKED BACK at a brisk pace. Erin soon felt the sweat trickling down her back, her shirt sticking to her. She licked her lips and tried not to think about how hot and thirsty she was.

"What's your plan when we find the panel?"

"Well, probably the first thing we should do, or, correction, *I* should do, is turn it off if it's on. Since the panel is leaking, we'll have to find a deep hole or cave to seal it in. Dr. Banushta will have to build a new toy if she wants a power panel to play with."

The path continued to climb steeply. Erin hadn't remembered the hills being quite this high.

"We're almost there, I think," said Noah. "I recognize that monolith."

"I'm glad you've been paying attention to our surroundings. I am completely lost—I can't even tell which stones are part of the path we are supposed to be following."

Climbing one last rocky incline, Erin spotted the cave where they had entered. She and Noah started searching the ground around its mouth.

They spread out, heads down, eyes scanning the sand.

"Noah! I found it!" Erin saw the black, flat rectangular panel sticking out of a pile of sand in front of her.

"Stop, Erin. Don't touch it. Let me get it."

Erin backed away from the panel, never taking her eyes off it. Erin pointed it out to him. But before he could get it, a triumphant figure dashed past them both and scooped the panel out of the sand, cradling it lovingly in her hands.

"Come to mother," said a gleeful Miranda.

"Dr. Banushta! What are you doing here?"

"I thought you were afraid to use the door," said Noah.

"I'm not afraid of anything," said Miranda haughtily. "I wanted someone else to do all the footwork for me, which you have both done very nicely."

"Dr. Banushta, the panel is dangerous," said

Noah. "It has almost killed Demont. Give it to me so I can dispose of it properly."

Dr. Banushta laughed at Noah. "I can fix this easily. Demont has done me a great favor with all his tinkering." She took off the back of the panel and looked confidently inside.

Noah stepped quickly forward intending to take the panel from her. Miranda whirled around and pointed the panel directly at Erin. "Leave me alone, or I'll send the Grimly-thing who knows where!"

Miranda fiddled with the panel, humming happily to herself.

"There. That should do it." She aimed the panel at the cave entrance and pushed a button. A steady stream of light particles beamed into the cave. Rocks crashed to the ground and dust billowed out of the mouth of the cave.

Miranda punched in another combination on the panel. "Goodbye," she waved and laughed at them.

"Dr. Banushta, wait. The panel has been damaged. You are taking a tremendous risk using it to transport yourself."

But Noah's words went unheeded. With a smirk, Miranda Banushta disappeared. The power panel, though, stayed behind, falling out of the air onto the sand.

"Boy, I'd like to see the look on her face when

she arrives empty-handed at her destination!" said Erin.

"I hope she made it to her destination," said Noah soberly. "I'm not letting another minute go by. This thing has got to go." He snatched the panel out of the sand and studied it carefully.

"Erin, get behind those rocks over there."

"What are you going to do?"

"I'm going to push every button on this thing and see if it will overload and self-destruct."

Erin ran for cover. She waved to Noah from her shelter behind the rocks.

"All set?" he called to her.

"All set!"

Erin held her breath as Noah proceeded to push all the buttons on the panel. She heard a low whine that grew louder and louder. Noah tossed the panel into the air and ran for cover. Three tremendous explosions rocked the area around them.

"I certainly got a bang out of that," said Noah with satisfaction.

"Very funny," said the deafened Erin. "Now what do we do?"

"We go back to the circle, I think."

They heard the sound of the shofar across the desert. Its eerie, mournful wail filled the vast expanse of sand. Erin started searching again for the trail. She called to Noah when she spotted it.

"Here's the trail."

But Noah was distracted, preoccupied, gazing into the late afternoon sky. Erin felt a longing coming from him, the same sense of homesickness she had felt coming from Demont.

"Noah, is something wrong?"

"What? Oh, no, no. I was just thinking . . . " His eyes were bright with tears.

"You . . . are you homesick? Are you missing heaven?" Erin asked softly, hesitantly.

Noah looked at her in astonishment. "I was! The sound of the shofar makes me think of . . . but how did you know?" He looked approvingly at Erin. "Your perceptive abilities are maturing."

"What is it like?" She looked in wonder at her friend almost as if she were seeing him for the first time.

"It is beyond description," he said, sighing with the memory.

"What do you miss the most?"

"Hmmm," Noah looked thoughtfully out across the barren expanse. "I really miss the green things right this minute," he laughed suddenly. "But I think I miss my breakfast conversations with the King and singing in the choir most of all."

"Will you and Mr. Gather be going back any time soon?" Erin asked the question, afraid Noah might say yes.

Noah looked at her and smiled. "Erin, Mr. Gather and I go back often, very often as a matter of fact. Being there doesn't mean we can't also be here with you. Heaven is a lot closer than you think." His eyes sparkled at her. "How about some music to make the walk more pleasant. Any requests?"

Erin thought for a minute. "You know what would be really appropriate? The part of "Amahl and the Night Visitors" where the three kings are coming to Amahl's house in the middle of the night. You can hear the camels walking in all the sand and everything."

Noah and Erin walked along, singing at various points in the music, the time and distance passing quickly. They reached the prayer plain again as the sun was setting.

17
The Calling

THE WIND WAS rising, the air colored a soft orange. Erin looked around her and marvelled at the natural beauty and majesty of the place. She wondered idly where the person who blew the shofar stood. Then she wondered where everyone else was.

"Noah, do you think Demont died?"

"No, Erin, look over there," Noah pointed to a turn in the path below them. Erin saw Protaimeus and Demont sitting together on a stone bench. Under the bench, Parenthesis sat meticulously licking her fur into place.

Noah and Erin moved to join them.

"How are you, Demont?" Erin looked with concern at the boy.

"Better, thank you," he answered, eyes downcast.

"Is he really?" Erin asked Protaimeus anxiously.

"Yes. He needed to be here, and he needed to be away from that panel." Protaimeus cleared his throat, looking out over the plain, casting sideways glances at Demont. Demont squirmed uncomfortably next to his guardian angel.

"Grimly-th—excuse me, Erin, I want . . . I mean I really . . . I'm sorry!" he said suddenly.

"About . . ." prompted Protaimeus gently.

"I'm sorry about all the trouble I've caused you and Mr. Sebastian, and everyone else."

"And . . ." said Protaimeus looking calmly at his young charge.

"And I am going to be different, better, from now on."

"Because . . ." prodded Protaimeus.

"I'm going to be different, better from now on, because . . ." Demont looked at Protaimeus who nodded encouragingly.

"Because today, when everyone was praying, I heard the Almighty call me—and I answered." Demont smiled shyly at Erin, looking her full in the face.

"The Almighty called *me*. He said 'Demont' right out loud. He knows my name." Demont was vibrant. "Imagine that! The King calling me!"

The last rays of the sun left the plain. Dusk settled all around. The wind sighed and moaned, whipping around Erin and Noah. Protaimeus's robe billowed out around him.

"It's time to go, Erin. Protaimeus, we need a new way home. Any suggestions?"

"Yes." Protaimeus got up to lead them.

"Is it far?" asked Erin.

"No, another entrance, or exit in this case, is quite near."

They walked together to the other side of the plain, and Erin caught a glimpse of sparkling azure.

"Protaimeus! Did I just see a flash of the lake at the oasis?"

"Yes, you did."

They walked down and around another smaller hill, and suddenly the oasis stretched out below them, invitingly cool and green. Protaimeus led them to a small tent set off by itself at the edge of camp.

"Walking into this tent will take you where you wish to go. We established this place of entry and exit after Erin's last visit here. The Almighty knew you would be back."

Protaimeus shook hands with Noah and Erin. "I am glad to see you again, Erin, and to meet your companion. It is wonderful that such good things have been accomplished. God go with you."

Erin and Noah turned to open the tent flap.

"Erin?" Demont's shy voice was almost a whisper.

She turned in surprise. "Yes?"

"I'd like to shake your hand, too."

Erin looked at Demont.

"But that will hurt you, won't it?" she asked.

"No, I don't think so, not anymore, because the King has spoken to me." Demont extended his hand awkwardly to Erin.

She reached out for his hand. His fingers touched hers and then grasped her hand in a firm grip. He started pumping it vigorously up and down. "You see," he said gleefully, "I *am* different now!"

The four of them said their goodbyes again, and Noah held the tent flap up so Erin could enter first. The dirt floor and the center pole certainly gave no clue as to an exit. Noah stepped into the tent, letting the flap fall shut behind him.

"Okay, Erin, you're the one with the explorer instincts. Where do we go from here?"

"You're asking me? I have no idea—wait a minute! I see another flap over there. My vote is to open it and see where it leads."

"Sounds good to me. Let's go."

In a matter of seconds, Noah and Erin stepped back into the shop. Mr. Gather and Arnold were sitting by the fireplace having a serious discussion.

"We're back!" Erin announced.

Her words were lost in the musical flurry of a french horn fanfare.

"It's not me this time!" A mystified Noah looked around the room.

"Those horns—we've heard them before, Erin," said Mr. Gather.

"I know! That's the fanfare that was played for Parenthesis's kittens! Do you suppose she's having some more?"

The horns played a heralding chorus again. A white dove flew into the room from the purple door. It dropped a small package and scroll at Erin's feet and flew away again.

"No, Erin, I don't think they are heralding the arrival of kittens this time," said Mr. Gather.

Erin picked up the box and scroll and came over to sit in her chair by the fire. She opened the scroll carefully.

"It's from High Council," she said excitedly. "Awarded to Erin Elizabeth Grimly for persistent compassion. God go with you." She looked puzzled. "Awarded? . . . "

Suddenly a flash of understanding crossed her face. Her hands trembled as she opened the little box. There, nestled in lavender tissue paper, was her guardian ring. She gently lifted it out and slid it on her finger. Then she started to laugh and cry.

Poor Arnold was completely in the dark. "Erin! What's wrong? What is it?"

Erin sniffed and laughed. "It's a long story, Arn."

Noah sat back in his chair, enjoying the moment. "I am so glad for you, Erin. I know how much this means to you."

"And, Erin Elizabeth Grimly, I know I speak for the whole circle of Guardians in High Council when I say how much it means to us that you have come this far."

Erin proudly studied the ring on her finger. "Thank you, Mr. Gather."

Arnold got up and walked over to the plants, the seriousness of the moment lost to him. "Hey, Mr. Gather, this is a nice tree you've got here." Arnold reached out to touch the trunk of Harold, the omnivorous conifer. A low growl from over his head caused him to jerk back.

"I wouldn't touch that tree if I were you, Arn," warned Erin. "That's Harold, a tree who eats *everything*." The clocks chiming six o'clock interrupted Erin's explanation.

"Oh, wow, I better get home. Mom's probably wondering where I am! Come on, Arn, I'll explain some of this to you on the way home, and the rest will just have to wait."

Noah and Mr. Gather saw them to the door. "Goodbye, Erin. Congratulations."

"God go with you, Erin, and with you Arnold."

"Thanks for everything, Mr. Gather, Mr. Sebastian." Arnold hesitated at the entrance. "Do you think I could come visit again? I really enjoyed talking to you today. I liked this place when it was a clubhouse, and well, I sort of miss it."

"Sure, Arnold, you're welcome anytime."

The two men watched the children go down the sidewalk and over the footbridge to Erin's backyard. They could hear the children's conversation.

"Let me see that ring you got, Erin."

Erin held up her hand for Arnold to see.

"Say, you know, that ring looks familiar. I think my uncle has one just like it!"

Epilogue

"Is not!"

"Is so!"

"IS NOT!"

"IS SO! Angels aren't supposed to argue, so you'd better hush," said Noah in a superior tone to his friend Sam.

"But Noah, be realistic. Arnold Lorenzo is not Guardian material. Anyone can see that. He's too . . . too . . . wishy-washy!"

Noah burst out laughing at Sam's description. "Well, wishy-washy or not, I think he may be our next project."

"What makes you think so?"

"Mr. Gather checked the Book today. Arnold's name is there."

Sam raised one eyebrow and whistled. "Just when I had hopes of a little vacation time."